A guide to the care &
feeding of your planet

Earthwise
at home

by Linda Lowery
and
Marybeth Lorbiecki

illustrated by
David Mataya

Carolrhoda Books, Inc./Minneapolis

Dear Reader, When you write to organizations listed in this book, please put two first-class stamps inside each envelope to pay for return postage. Also include a note with your name and address on it. Don't worry if it takes four to six weeks for an answer. Remember, too, that if your friends and classmates all write to different organizations, you can share the information you receive (and that saves paper and trees!).

This book is dedicated to each of you who takes that extra moment to crush a can, turn off a light, or pick up a bottle in the sand. — LL

To my grandmother Dorothy Schneider, who has been conserving and reusing from way back, and for the next generation, which gives me hope — most especially my godson Alex Moher, Emily Moher, and the beautiful Nelson gals, Rachel, Sarah, and Grace. — MbL

Special thanks to those individuals and organizations who aided in research and verification of facts: Betty Botts, Rachel Oppelt and Gale Turner at Environment Canada, Chicago Park District Recycling, Earthtrust, Eco-Cycle, Hennepin County Recycling, National Center for Atmospheric Research, National Wildlife Federation, Solar and Electric Car Racing Association, Student Conservation Association, Neighborhood Energy Consortium, World Resources Institute, and World Watch Institute. Kudos and thanks to designer Kirsten Ford, photo researcher Colleen Sexton, Emily Kelley, Jim Simondet, Gary Hansen, Jill Anderson, Michael Tacheny, Steve Woods, and Jessie Lohman.

METRIC CONVERSION CHART		
To find measurements that are almost equal		
WHEN YOU KNOW:	**MULTIPLY BY:**	**TO FIND:**
AREA		
acres	0.41	hectares
square miles	2.59	square kilometers
CAPACITY		
gallons	3.79	liters
LENGTH		
feet	30.48	centimeters
yards	0.91	meters
miles	1.61	kilometers
MASS (weight)		
pounds	0.45	kilograms
tons	0.91	metric tons
VOLUME		
cubic yards	0.77	cubic meters
TEMPERATURE degrees Fahrenheit	(subtract 32 and then) 0.56	degrees Celsius

Library of Congress
Cataloging-in-Publication Data

Lowery, Linda
  Earthwise at home: a guide to the care & feeding of your planet/ by Linda Lowery and Marybeth Lorbiecki; illustrated by David Mataya.
     p.   cm.
  Includes index.
  Summary: Suggests activities that can help save our planet. Including recycling, power conservation, and smart shopping.
  ISBN 0-87614-730-9 (lib. bdg.)
  ISBN 0-87614-585-3 (pbk.)
  1. Environmental protection—Citizen participation—Juvenile literature. 2. Environmental protection—United States—Citizen participation—Juvenile literature. [Environmental protection.]
I. Lorbiecki, Marybeth. II. Mataya, David, ill. III. Title.
TD171.7.I69   1993
363.7'0525—dc20   93-1332
                                CIP
                                 AC
Manufactured in the United States
          of America
1 2 3 4 5 6 98 97 96 95 94 93

Text copyright © 1993 by Linda Lowery and Marybeth Lorbiecki
Illustrations copyright © 1993 by David Mataya

Printed on recycled, recyclable, acid-free paper.

This book is available in two editions:
Library binding by
Carolrhoda Books, Inc.
Soft cover by First Avenue Editions
241 First Avenue North
Minneapolis, MN 55401

A teachers' guide is also available through Carolrhoda Books, Inc.

A guide to the care &
feeding of your planet

Earthwise
at home

by Linda Lowery
and
Marybeth Lorbiecki

illustrated by
David Mataya

Carolrhoda Books, Inc./Minneapolis

Dear Reader, When you write to organizations listed in this book, please put two first-class stamps inside each envelope to pay for return postage. Also include a note with your name and address on it. Don't worry if it takes four to six weeks for an answer. Remember, too, that if your friends and classmates all write to different organizations, you can share the information you receive (and that saves paper and trees!).

This book is dedicated to each of you who takes that extra moment to crush a can, turn off a light, or pick up a bottle in the sand. —LL

To my grandmother Dorothy Schneider, who has been conserving and reusing from way back, and for the next generation, which gives me hope — most especially my godson Alex Moher, Emily Moher, and the beautiful Nelson gals, Rachel, Sarah, and Grace. —MbL

Special thanks to those individuals and organizations who aided in research and verification of facts: Betty Botts, Rachel Oppelt and Gale Turner at Environment Canada, Chicago Park District Recycling, Earthtrust, Eco-Cycle, Hennepin County Recycling, National Center for Atmospheric Research, National Wildlife Federation, Solar and Electric Car Racing Association, Student Conservation Association, Neighborhood Energy Consortium, World Resources Institute, and World Watch Institute. Kudos and thanks to designer Kirsten Ford, photo researcher Colleen Sexton, Emily Kelley, Jim Simondet, Gary Hansen, Jill Anderson, Michael Tacheny, Steve Woods, and Jessie Lohman.

METRIC CONVERSION CHART To find measurements that are almost equal		
WHEN YOU KNOW:	**MULTIPLY BY:**	**TO FIND:**
AREA		
acres	0.41	hectares
square miles	2.59	square kilometers
CAPACITY		
gallons	3.79	liters
LENGTH		
feet	30.48	centimeters
yards	0.91	meters
miles	1.61	kilometers
MASS (weight)		
pounds	0.45	kilograms
tons	0.91	metric tons
VOLUME		
cubic yards	0.77	cubic meters
TEMPERATURE degrees Fahrenheit	(subtract 32 and then) 0.56	degrees Celsius

Library of Congress
Cataloging-in-Publication Data

Lowery, Linda
Earthwise at home: a guide to the care & feeding of your planet/ by Linda Lowery and Marybeth Lorbiecki; illustrated by David Mataya.
p. cm.
Includes index.
Summary: Suggests activities that can help save our planet. Including recycling, power conservation, and smart shopping.
ISBN 0-87614-730-9 (lib. bdg.)
ISBN 0-87614-585-3 (pbk.)
1. Environmental protection—Citizen participation—Juvenile literature. 2. Environmental protection—United States—Citizen participation—Juvenile literature. [Environmental protection.]
I. Lorbiecki, Marybeth. II. Mataya, David, ill. III. Title.
TD171.7.169 1993
363.7'0525–dc20   93-1332
                                                     CIP
                                                     AC

Manufactured in the United States of America

1 2 3 4 5 6 98 97 96 95 94 93

Printed on recycled, recyclable, acid-free paper.

This book is available in two editions:
Library binding by Carolrhoda Books, Inc.
Soft cover by First Avenue Editions
241 First Avenue North
Minneapolis, MN 55401

A teachers' guide is also available through Carolrhoda Books, Inc.

Contents

Photograph Acknowledgements
Front cover: © Frances M. Roberts. Back cover: © Richard
B. Levine. © Frances M. Roberts, p. 3; Heidi B. Lovett/
Center for Marine Conservation, 5; Ohio Department of
Natural Resources, 7, 23 left; Environment Canada, 9;
Jim Simondet, 10, 14, 15; Solar Survival Architecture, 11
left; Christine Simpson, 11 right; © David Falconer, 13;
Department of Environmental Quality, 16; Wisconsin
Department of Natural Resources, 17, 27 right; Chicago
Park District, 18; Scientific Certification Systems Green
Cross, 21; Minnesota Water Pollution Control Authority,
22; Independent Picture Service, 23 left; Hank Andrews/
Visuals Unlimited, 23 right; Minneapolis Public Library
and Information Center, 24 left, 26-27, 29 right; U.S. Fish
and Wildlife, 24 right; U.S. Department of Agriculture, 29
left; Merlin D. Tuttle/Bat Conservation International, 31;
Chesapeake Bay Foundation, 34; British Tourist Authority,
36; Jerry Miller/Northern States Power Company, 37;
Joseph L. Fontenot/Visuals Unlimited, 39; James H.
Carmichael, 41; Marybeth Lorbiecki, 43; Earthtrust/
Flipper Foundation, 44; Maine Heritage Trust, p. 47.

This
is
Our
Earth
And we want it back
From the Polluters
Anthony Valenti

What Does
Earthwise Mean?

Have you heard about the bad things happening to the earth—oil spills, garbage piles, air pollution, poisoned rivers, and things like that? Don't let them get you down. There are things each one of us can do to make the planet healthier. And we can do them wherever we are —in our apartments or houses, our classrooms or schoolyards, our neighborhood parks or county woods.

First we need to find out as much information as we can about how the earth works. Then we will be able to take actions that make sense for the whole planet—actions that are *earthwise*. Sometimes these actions will be fun and easy to do. Sometimes they will be hard. There will even be times when it will be difficult to decide what's the best thing to do. But that's okay. There are always many ways to look at a problem, and it usually takes time to sort out all the facts and possible solutions. We often have to try a few solutions to see which ones work the best.

earthwise

You can begin your *earthwise* search here. Learn how the things we do at home help or hurt the planet. Then try picking an *earth-wise* project to do. See if your family wants to join in. Don't worry about not being able to do everything at once. We have our whole lives to learn how to be more *earth-wise* each day.

Trashing Out

Garbage, Garbage, Everywhere

Look around your home. Doesn't it seem like almost everything you do makes garbage? There are food scraps, cans, bottles, containers, and wrappings left after you eat.

There are sheets of paper left after you do your homework. There are broken games and toys. There are clothes you've outgrown and books you no longer read. Then look at your friends' homes. They probably have the same problems.

The average person in the United States makes almost 4½ pounds of garbage every day. In Canada each person makes a little less—3¾ pounds per day. This means that each of us throws away between 1,300 and 1,600 pounds of garbage each year. That's more than the weight of 25 second graders. And there are about 279 million people in these two countries. Imagine everyone making that much garbage every day, every year!

IT ALL ADDS UP

Try an experiment with your friends. For one weekend, put all the food, bottles, bags, wrappers, and other things you want to throw away in your own bag or basket. (Weigh the bag or basket first.) Then at the end of the weekend, weigh the bag or basket with all the garbage in it. Subtract the weight of the container.

How many pounds of trash did you make? Was it less or more than your friends made? Was it less or more than the national average? Isn't it amazing how quickly garbage adds up?

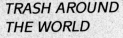

SPACE MESS

There is even trash in space. The countries that have sent satellites and rockets into space have left their mark on our galaxy. Parts of spacecrafts, chips of paint, and even tools have been left behind. Scientists think that over 30,000 bits of garbage are now orbiting the earth. If a speeding spaceship hits just one floating sliver of trash, the ship will be damaged.

TRASH AROUND THE WORLD

Not everybody in the world makes as much garbage a day as people in the U.S. and Canada. Here are the averages for some other countries:

Ghana	½ pound
Egypt	¾ pound
Sri Lanka	¾ pound
Philippines	1 pound
Japan	1¾ pounds
Sweden	2 pounds

People in poorer countries usually make less garbage than people in richer countries because they buy fewer things and they reuse more of them.

WHAT'S IT ALL ABOUT?

Each year Americans toss away at least:

- 12 billion pounds of food scraps
- 28 billion glass bottles and jars
- 25 billion foam cups (enough to circle the earth 436 times)
- 90 billion plastic bottles
- 18 billion disposable diapers
- 62 billion pounds of paper
- 200 million tires

Crushed together, Americans' garbage makes a 344-billion-pound mountain of solid waste. If you made this waste into blocks 1 yard wide, 1 yard long, and 1 yard tall, and then stacked them one on top of the other, you would have a column that reached to the moon (and 76,000 miles beyond it)! And this is just one year's garbage from one country.

Where Does It All End Up?

Most garbage is carted straight
from trash cans to huge holes
in the ground.
These holes are called landfills.
The garbage is dumped in, covered
with dirt, and left there to rot.
But much of it never rots.
It just sits in landfills forever.
If a landfill is handled carelessly,
poisonous gases can build up and
leak into the ground, air, and water.
Sometimes bad odors leak out too.
Can you see why people don't like
to live near landfills?

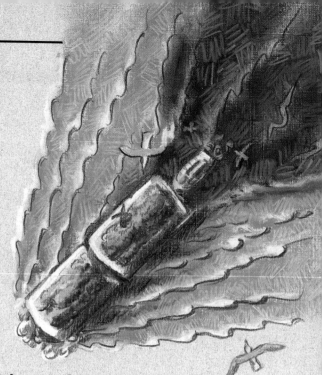

Other garbage is taken
on barges out into the ocean,
where it is dumped.
The garbage floats to the shore
or sinks to the bottom.
Shorebirds and animals
sometimes eat the garbage
and die.
Thick layers of sludge build up
on the ocean floor.
The sludge kills
the animals and plants
that live there.
Still other garbage is burned.
Its smoke puts poisonous gases
into the air we breathe.

Sometimes the poisons
in the air mix with rain.
When the rain falls,
the poisons harm
plants, animals,
lakes, rivers,
and soil.

BATTERIES CAN BE DANGEROUS JUNK

Most families in the U.S. toss out at least eight batteries a year. Each battery has poison in it. The poison can leak into the water, ground, and air when it is thrown away. If you don't want to worry about this, pick toys that don't use batteries. Or use a battery recharger. If you have dead batteries, bring them to a drop-off center (call your city or county office for the location), or take them back to the store where you bought them.

None of these ways
to take care of garbage
seem very good, do they?
That's why many people are
looking for better solutions
to our garbage problems.

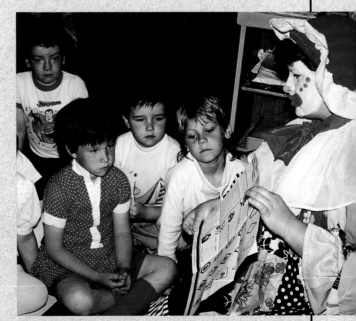

Children in a Canadian park learn about different kinds of garbage and what happens to them after they are thrown away.

Maybe There's No Such Thing as Garbage

One of the first things each of us can do is ask:
Just what is garbage?
Garbage is anything
that can't be used.
Yet there are very few things
in this world that can't be used
for something.
Leftover food can be
turned into soil.
Dirty cans can be
made into new cans.
Used bottles and jars can be
cleaned and filled again.
Worn tires can be made
into shoes, purses,
and new tires. Thrown-
away plastics can
be crushed to make
building materials.
Used chemicals can be
sorted and reused.
Old paper can be made
into new paper.

So as you can see, garbage is really one of the world's greatest resources! People around the globe— scientists, inventors, and even kids—are constantly coming up with new, exciting ways to use our trash.

FIX IT

Many things that are thrown away could be fixed instead: torn clothes, broken toys, bent tools, furniture. Often if you take something apart carefully, you learn how it works. Look through the broken things you own. Instead of tossing them away, take them apart with an adult, and figure out how they work. You may be surprised at how good you are at fixing things.

EARTHSHIPS

Have you ever heard of a house made out of trash? In New Mexico, some homes are called "Earthships." On the outside, they look like some adobe clay homes. But whole tires and soda cans are built into their thick walls. During the day, the walls soak up the sun's heat. At night, the trash in the walls holds in the heat and keeps the people in the house warm. Earthships use up garbage and save energy.

OVER AND OVER AGAIN

People used to think it was good to be able to use something once and then throw it away. Now they realize what a waste that is. Why buy something disposable if you can buy something that will last a long time? Then you can enjoy it over and over again.

SEWAGE TO FERTILIZER

Some cities are finding out that sewage can be worth money. Large treatment machines strain the city's raw sewage and remove the poisons from it. Then the sewage is treated to make it safe and odorless. The cities sell the treated sewage as fertilizer. Farmers and home gardeners can use this natural fertilizer instead of chemical fertilizers. There are also toilets that can make sewage into fertilizer right in your own home.

Refusing

Some of these new ways to reuse our trash can't be done in our homes.

So the best way we can reduce the amount of unused garbage in the world is to refuse to make any more garbage than we have to. Here are some ways we can make a little less trash every week.

CUT THE PAPER

We waste more paper than anything else. Start a contest in your home to see who can come up with the most ideas to stop wasting paper. Here are some to start you off: Use washable cups and plates instead of paper cups and plates. Cut up large squares of cloth and make them into reusable dishcloths, towels, and napkins. (You can make napkin rings out of papier-mâché, wood, or clay.) Carry handkerchiefs instead of tissues.

HEAVY WRAP

Each month Americans throw away their weight in packaging. That's a lot of boxes, bags, and wrappers! Sometimes the packages are two or three times bigger than what you are buying. You can encourage stores and factories to use less packaging by choosing things with little or no packaging. Letters to local businesses or government leaders might help other people think about packaging too.

YOU CAN SAY NO TO UNWANTED MAIL

A lot of people don't like all the ads they get in the mail. They often call them junk mail. It has been said that Americans spend about eight months of their lives reading unwanted catalogs and advertising. Do you want to waste that much time? Or that many trees? Each year 100 million trees are used to make the paper for junk mail.

To stop unwanted mail from coming to your home, write a postcard to the companies that are sending you things and ask them to take you off their mailing lists. You can also write to:

Mail Preference Service c/o
Direct Marketing Association
11 W. 42nd Street
P.O. Box 3861
New York, NY 10163-3861

NEED OR WANT?

If you were being sent off to the moon to live for a week and could take only 20 things with you, what would you take? Would you take Mom or Dad? Something to wear? Things to eat? Or drink?

The first thing to do is decide: What do I need to live? And then: What extra things do I want to take along to make my stay more fun? These are the differences between things you need and things you want. Needs are necessary to live. Wants are extras for pleasure. So the next time you go to the store and think you need something, think again. Is it a need? Or a want? Things that are wants are usually wrapped up in the most packaging, and they are the easiest to live without.

Reusing

What do we do if we already have something we don't want and we can't figure out how to use it? Should we throw it away? No way!

JUNKYARD ART

A man near Baraboo, Wisconsin, runs a junkyard and sculpture garden. He has made his money by collecting and selling things that other people thought were useless. Now he takes screws, nuts, bolts, wrought-iron, barrels, wheels, tools, and motors, and he turns them into enormous sculptures. Robots, machines, and giant hearts decorate his yard. You can buy some of his works of art. Or you can buy some of his junk by the pound to make your own.

ALWAYS A BORROWER AND A LENDER BE

If someone wants to use one of your toys or books, why not lend it out? Then if you'd like to borrow something sometime, you can ask others to lend it to you. Sharing with others is often twice the fun.

A junkyard dog made by a ten-year-old boy and welded together by his father

ONE PERSON'S TRASH IS ANOTHER'S TREASURE

The things you don't want may be just the things someone else is looking for. Make hand-me-downs out of them. Give them to the Salvation Army, Goodwill, a homeless shelter, or a missionary group. Or put a low price on them, and sell them at a yard sale.

WRAP IT UP

Each year Americans throw away $300 million worth of wrapping paper. Next time you get a present, save the paper and ribbon for the next gift you give. Or wrap the gift in a bright piece of cloth that can be used and reused. Or make your own wrapping out of old Sunday comics. You can also decorate brown bags with original designs. Cut potatoes in half. Then cut the halves into shapes, such as hearts, stars, or trees. Dip the potatoes in paint and make colorful prints on the paper.

SCARY!

Did you know that ½ of all the plastic Halloween costumes bought each year are used only once? That's a lot of plastic garbage. Instead of buying a costume, why not make your own? Torn sheets make great ghosts. Old plastic bags can be cut open and made into capes, gowns, or space suits. Use ripped jeans and an old shirt to become a scarecrow, beach bum, or rock star. With makeup, you can be anything from a vampire to a clown to a nasty witch.

Recycling

Okay, you've fixed, given away,
or made new things out
of everything you can.
What do you do now?
RECYCLE!
To recycle means
to remake something
into a brand new object.
Factories can melt down glass
jars and bottles to make new
glass containers.

Metal objects, such as cans,
can be melted down
and made into new cans.
Used paper is soaked, filtered,
and remixed into new paper.
Chemicals, tires, plastics, and oil
are reworked and used again.
More and more materials are
being recycled all the time.

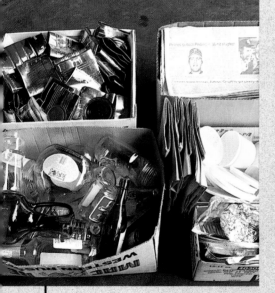

READY, SET, GO
*Set up a recycling center in
your home. Line up paper bags,
cardboard boxes, or plastic recycling
bins in an out-of-the-way place. On each
container, make a sign saying what should go in it:
glass, metal, paper, cardboard, or plastic.*

*Some cities want glass sorted by color. Others want
newspapers separate from magazines, catalogs, junk
mail, telephone books, and other kinds of paper.*

*Once your recycling center is set up, your family is
ready to go. Rinse all cans, bottles, and jars. Flatten all cans, cardboard, and
plastic containers. Toss them in their places. Keep batteries and strong-smelling
chemical liquids, such as paint, oil, or ammonia, in a separate place. There should
be special drop-off centers for these items in your neighborhood. If your area
doesn't have drop-off centers or a recycling program, write the leaders of your
city and county to ask them why you don't.*

Recycling Pays

TRASH TO CASH

Many people collect the cans and bottles that have been left on sidewalks or streets. They take these to recycling companies and get paid for them. In some states, glass bottles can also be taken back to stores for deposits. So next time you're looking for extra money, try picking up some litter.

JUICING IT UP

Kids in the U.S. throw away more than four billion little drink boxes a year. Drink boxes can sit for 300 to 400 years in a landfill. As an answer to this problem, some cities and school systems have drink-box recycling programs. If there isn't a drink-box recycling program in your area, ask your student council to start one. Better yet, try filling a thermos or sports bottle with juice instead of buying drink boxes—and urge your friends to do the same.

RECYCLING SUCCESS STORY

Out of 83 billion aluminum cans now made each year in the U.S., almost all have some recycled material in them. Over ½ of these cans are recycled again after they are used.

TRASHY TRIVIA

• More than 75% of all garbage in the U.S. can be recycled. But only 15% of the garbage is now being recycled.
• Over ½ of landfill garbage is paper. If we recycled 1 out of 10 newspapers, we would save 25 million trees every year.

WHAT'S YOUR NUMBER?

Since plastics come in different mixtures and weights, they are sorted before they are melted. To keep them straight, the types of plastic are numbered one through seven. (The numbers are generally found on the bottom of the plastic items.) Number 1 plastics are often used for drink containers (usually clear or green). Number 2 plastics are usually used for milk, water, soap, or bleach containers (usually white or a solid color). These two plastics are the easiest kinds to recycle. Although more and more plastics can be recycled, this still does not solve all of the problems with plastics. A lot of dangerous chemicals are used in making and recycling them. So the less we "need" and use plastics, the better.

PLASTIC PLAYGROUNDS

How do plastic milk jugs and pop bottles keep Chicago kids safer while they play? The children bring their plastic trash to their neighborhood parks. Then it is sent out to be recycled into plastic wood. The wood is used to build safety walls around playgrounds. Since 1990 almost 300 Chicago playgrounds have been enclosed by kids' trash. Plastic can also be recycled into park benches, tennis balls, carpet, toys, and tennis shoes.

MELT THAT PEANUT

Those squiggly white packing peanuts used to sit in landfills forever. That was because they were made of foam. Now some businesses use peanuts made of cornstarch. Just run handfuls of them under water, and watch them dissolve!

RECYCLE YOUR OWN PAPER

1 Take several sheets of paper out of your home recycling center. (The paper can be plain or colored.) Rip the sheets into tiny pieces. Place them in a bucket of water to soak overnight.

2 Find an old, framed window screen. (Or take cheesecloth, muslin, or burlap, and stretch it TIGHTLY over an old picture frame, tacking or stapling the cloth to the frame.) Put the screen over a tub or sink.

3 Use an eggbeater to chop and mix up the soaked paper. A blender works well too. When done, the mixture should look like creamy soup. (If the mixture is too thick to mix well, add more water.)

4 Pour the paper soup onto the screen, and spread the mixture out thinly and evenly. Let it drip. Place a few sheets of newspaper over the mixture. Smooth down the newspapers, pressing out the water.

5 Flip the screen over onto a large cookie sheet (with the newspaper side down). Remove the screen. Cover the top of the mixture with sheets of newspaper. Press more water out.

6 When as much water as possible has been patted or pressed out, gently pull off the newspapers from the top. Place a piece of waxed paper over the mixture. Flip the cookie sheet over again (with waxed paper side down) onto an out-of-the-way counter, table, or place on the floor.

7 Gently remove the cookie sheet and layer of newspapers. Let the paper mixture dry overnight on the waxed paper. The next day you will have a beautiful, unique, handmade sheet of paper.

SAY CHEESE, PLEASE

Americans use about 7,000 plastic bottles every second. Plastic takes a long time to rot, if it rots at all. But now a new kind of plastic is being made out of potato peels and cheese leftovers. This plastic is made of natural ingredients, so it can rot and become part of the soil.

Taking Care of the Leftovers

After we've reused and recycled as much of our trash as we can, what's left?

Food scraps, grass, leaves, weeds, and wood—that's what. These natural things rot over time. They spoil and break down into tiny pieces that are eaten by animals and small organisms. Eventually these pieces become part of the soil. Things that rot like this are called biodegradable.

You can help biodegradable objects become new soil by composting.

Composting means putting natural things in a pile outdoors and helping them rot.

You can make your own compost pile.

Or you can bring your family's biodegradable items to a compost pile run by your neighborhood or county.

THE EARTHWISE EARTHWORM

Do you know how the earthworm got its name? It eats the leaves and dead plants on the ground. Then its body recycles the waste so it becomes a part of the soil. An earthworm really IS a worm that makes earth!

WILL IT ROT, OR NOT?

Some plastic products or packaging are called biodegradable. But most times they are not. It usually takes 500 years of sitting in the sun for these so-called "biodegradable" plastics to break down. And since most of them end up buried in a landfill, they never see a ray of sunlight.

MAKE YOUR OWN
SOIL FACTORY

Inside your home, collect all food scraps (except meat and bones) in a tightly covered waste basket. Outside, collect all leaves, grass clippings, or weeds in a wire, wooden, or plastic box with slats. Once a week, pour the food scraps into the outside box, and have someone stir the pile with a rake.

In a month you'll be able to feel heat coming from your compost pile. In a year you'll have new soil for your potted plants, windowboxes, gardens, lawns, or trees. If you live in an apartment, ask the caretaker to start a compost pile for everyone. For more directions on composting, go to the library or a gardening store.

Once you have composted everything that's biodegradable, you might find that you still have some trashy leftovers: some plastics, metals, and other materials that can't be recycled. These must be thrown away. For now.
But maybe by the time you're an adult, there won't be anything left that isn't biodegradable, recyclable, or reusable.

LONG-TIME LITTER

This is the time it takes for some kinds of litter to biodegrade:

banana peels	2-5 wks.
paper	2-12 mos.
milk cartons	5 yrs.
cigarette butts	12 yrs.
plastic bags	20-30 yrs.
leather shoes	25-50 yrs.
aluminum cans	200-500 yrs.
disposable diapers	300-500 yrs.
plastic 6-pack rings	450 yrs.
plastic foam	never

YOU CAN'T FOOL ME!

Some businesses write things on product labels that make people think their products are good for the environment. So scientists at an organization called Green Cross test products to see if businesses are telling the truth. If they are, Green Cross puts a seal of approval on the products' labels. This seal keeps you from being fooled.

S.C.S.
GREEN
CROSS

Water Waste

Not a Drop to Drink

If there weren't water on the earth, we couldn't live here. Everything alive needs water— water to drink, water to wash with, water to live in.

But the earth is facing a big problem. Every day our water is getting dirtier. Fertilizers, factory chemicals, soil, cleaners, paint, and oil are harming our rivers, lakes, oceans, swamps, and underground wells.

How do these materials get into the water? They are dumped or spilled there. They are washed there by rain. They are piped there by sewage plants.

Can we stop our water from getting dirtier and start cleaning it up? You bet!

WARNING

THIS WATER UNSUITABLE FOR SWIMMING, DRINKING, AND WADING. CITY OF LITTLE ROCK

WATER SICKNESS

In 1983 some kids in Whately, Massachusetts, started getting strange rashes on their skin. The city found out that chemicals from nearby potato and tobacco fields had washed into their water supply. The chemicals were making people sick. So the people in the city got together to dig a new well to find clean, safe water. They also worked to stop the use of chemicals on the surrounding farm fields. For information on how to keep your water safe, your family can write to:

Citizens Clearinghouse
for Hazardous Wastes
P.O. Box 6806
Falls Church, VA 22040

THE RIVER'S BURNING!

On June 22, 1969, the Cuyahoga River in Cleveland, Ohio, went up in flames. The river caught fire because it was so polluted. The river had been ablaze before, but this fire made people realize something had to be done. They started working to stop the dumping of chemicals and sewage into the river. Today the Cuyahoga River is healthier. Downstream from Cleveland, the river attracts insects and birds. The river around Cleveland, however, still needs more work.

SOME GRASS-ROOTS TIPS

• Some people with lawns and gardens put up to 10 times more chemicals on their soil per acre than farmers do. Just a little of these chemicals can make animals sick. That's why more and more gardening stores are selling fertilizers and bug sprays that are natural. They are biodegradable and are not poisonous.

• Many people use up clean water by putting it on their lawns. Instead, they can plant grasses that don't need as much water. And when they cut the lawn, they can leave the clippings on it.

• Push mowers are perfect lawn tools. They are quiet and safe, they don't use gas, and they aren't any more work than an upright power mower.

• If you'd like to receive a free brochure with more tips for earthwise lawn and garden care, write to:

Rodale Press
Organic Gardening
33 East Minor Street
Emmaus, PA 18098

A STICKY SITUATION

One pint of crankcase oil can make a one-acre oil spill. So if you ever help someone change the oil or antifreeze in a motor, remind the person not to pour the liquids down the drain. Take them to a gas station or drop-off center

Down the Drain

Saving the earth's water
is a job everyone can do.
Even you.
There are two ways you can help:
don't waste clean water
(conserve it!) and
don't pour dangerous things
down the drain.

WASHING WITH LESS

Q: *Which uses less water, washing a bike with a hose or with a sponge and bucket?*

A: *A sponge and bucket. With a hose, it usually takes about 30 gallons. The bucket method generally takes only 2. To clean a car, it often takes 150 gallons with a hose — but only 15 with a bucket. That means you can wash a bike or a car 10 times with a sponge and bucket before you use the same amount of water you would use once with a hose.*

DRIPPY FACTS

• *A dripping faucet wastes 300 to 4,000 gallons of water per month.*

• *When you take a bath, you use three times more water than when you shower. New efficient shower heads use even less water.*

• *If your toilet is broken and runs all the time, it can waste 50 gallons a day without any flushing.*

• *Each of us uses about 35 gallons of water a day just flushing the toilet. But you can cut down on that water. Take a plastic bottle and fill it with sand. With the help of an adult, place it in the tank of your toilet. This makes the toilet use less water. From now until next year, you'll save thousands of gallons of water.*

BRUSHING UP

Q: How many gallons of water do you think you waste when you brush your teeth with the water running?

A: Five. If you brush twice a day, that's 3,650 gallons a year. That's enough water to fill up a bathtub 150 times. So turn off the water while you are brushing, and you can save enough water for a whole year of baths.

OLD PIPES

Some pipes in older buildings are made of lead. If lead gets into our drinking water, it can be harmful to us. So if you live or go to school in an old building, let the water run for about a minute before filling up your glass for a drink. This flushes out the pipes. Catch the extra water in a jar or watering can and use it to water your houseplants (not your vegetables). And at your yearly checkup, have the doctor see that your body is safe from lead.

CLEANING UP CLEANERS

Think of all those cans and bottles of smelly liquids people use for cleaning. If they smell bad, they're probably dangerous. Many paints, nail polishes, film chemicals, oils, and drain decloggers are also deadly. If you pour them down the sink, they'll end up poisoning water somewhere. So you might want to try natural cleaners instead. A mixture of vinegar and water is one of the best all-around cleaners.

For other tips, write to:
Greenpeace
1432 U Street Northwest
Washington, DC 20009
Ask for the free flyer—
Stepping Lightly on the Earth:
Everyone's Guide to Toxins in
the Home.

Something in the Air

Air Raid

Just as the water in our world
is getting dirtier, so is the air.
Cars, planes, factories, and
garbage burners leak poisonous
smoke into the skies.
Spray cans, air conditioners,
and refrigerators give off unseen
chemicals that harm the earth.
Zooming planes, frightening
gunshots, grinding machines,
humming computers, ringing
telephones, and blaring TVs
fill the air.
All this noise can harm
our hearing and disturb wildlife.
So what can we do?
We can do our best to keep
    the air around us clean, safe,
      and even once in a while
        quiet.

GET FRESH

*Winter and summer, it's important
to open your windows for some time
each day. Many things in your home,
such as carpets, hair sprays, and
cleaners, put invisible particles into
the air. By opening the window, you
keep these particles from filling up your
home and your lungs. This airing out
also helps keep molds and fungi from
growing in your home. (They love
heating and air-conditioning systems.)*

HELPFUL HOUSEPLANTS

*Plants can really dress up a room. But in some
ways, they can clean it too. Plants take in dirty
air and clean it before giving it off again.
Even if you live in a place with no windows,
you can still grow plants. There are now
lightbulbs that make light like sunlight. These
bulbs can be bought at some of the stores
listed in the back of this book.*

SMELLY BUSINESS

Experiment with smells. When you come home from school, close your eyes as you open the door. What do you smell? Can you tell what's for dinner? Does the cat litter need to be changed? Is someone chewing gum? Are there flowers in the house?

Then try going for a walk in a park, through the woods, or near a pond. Close your eyes again. Can you smell wet leaves? Can you tell if it's going to rain or snow? Many animals depend mostly on their sense of smell to find food or get away from enemies. Do you think smoke or chemicals in the air make it harder for animals to smell things?

SILENCE STALKER

Is silence really hard to find? Visit quiet places (under your blankets, a closet, a park) and see for yourself. Close your eyes and count the different sounds you hear. Can you connect the sounds with the things that make them? Were you able to find a place where you couldn't hear anything?

SMOKING POLLUTES

Chris Warner of Lake Mills, Wisconsin, was nine when he decided to help clean up the air. He began in his own home. Chris told his mom that each cigarette she smoked took eight minutes off her life. The smoke hurt her lungs and Chris's too. And the cigarette butts made litter. Chris begged his mom to quit smoking. "There will still be pollution," said Chris, "but there will be less."

There's a Hole in the Sky

The chemicals we put into the air
can cause problems in places
we can't even see.
Miles above us, the earth is
surrounded by a layer
of gas called ozone.
This ozone blanket works like
a sun shade for our planet.
It protects us from the sun's rays
that are too hot and too bright.
Without ozone, these sun rays
could burn our skin,
shrivel up crops, melt glaciers,
and change the weather.

The ozone blanket is getting
thinner year by year.
There is a hole in the ozone
over the South Pole,
and a hole over the North Pole.
Chemicals we put into the air
help make these holes.
Every day, scientists are learning
more about how we can stop
using these chemicals and
protect our ozone blanket.

SAFE SUBSTITUTES
*If your family would like to
know about specific products
that are kind or harmful to
the ozone layer, they
can write to:*
The Environmental
Defense Fund
Publications
257 Park Ave. S.
New York, NY 10010

The National Toxics
Campaign Fund
1168 Common-
wealth Ave.
Boston, MA
02134

*The pollution caused by the
blast-off of satellites and
space ships is very destructive
to the ozone layer.*

TINY VILLAINS

Scientists believe the main villains making holes in the ozone blanket are tiny chemicals with big names. They are called chlorofluorocarbons or CFCs. CFCs and many of their chemical relatives destroy ozone. They are used to make certain kinds of plastic foam, computers, televisions, refrigerators, air conditioners, and aerosol sprays. Scientists are hard at work to find harmless substitutes for CFCs and their relatives. Many countries have signed an agreement to stop using CFCs completely by the year 2000. Write to your government leaders and ask if your country has signed the agreement.

CFC ROUNDUP

Q: What can you do to protect the ozone blanket?
A: Buy only "ozone-friendly" products.
• Avoid products in aerosol cans, including plastic string, hair sprays, spray paints, furniture polishes, spot removers, and cleaners for VCRs and stereos. Use pump sprays instead.
• Try not to buy anything made of (or packaged in) foam plastic or foam rubber. If you do, recycle them.
• If your refrigerator or air conditioner dies, remind your parents to bring it to a used appliance store or a drop-off center. If these appliances are left in a dump, the CFCs in the coils might escape.

LONG-NAMED SIDEKICK

Another villain robbing the ozone is methyl chloroform. Its product name is 1,1,1 trichloroethane. Keep this long-named thief out of your home!

Bug Off!

Which is worse, to live with bugs
or to live with pollution?
Some people think bugs are worse.
So they use poisonous sprays
and powders to kill mosquitoes,
termites, ants, and cockroaches.
These chemicals are very harmful
to breathe or eat.
But there are other ways
to get rid of pests—
and still not pollute.

GARLIC'S GREAT

Most insects stay clear of garlic. So one way to keep insects from coming into your rooms and cupboards is to grate a lot of garlic and put it into water in an old spray bottle. Spray this mixture into cracks and corners. Or sprinkle a powder of hot pepper. For ants, use fresh mint. For cockroaches, seal up cracks and corners as best you can and then use a garlic spray and a hot-pepper powder. Flyswatters and flypaper work well for flies. For more natural tips on keeping bugs away, write to:
National Coalition
Against the Misuse of
Pesticides (NCAMP)
701 E Street Southeast
Washington, DC 20003

DON'T EAT MY HOUSE!

Termites in Florida and California eat up $120 million worth of wooden homes every year. To avoid using dangerous sprays, scientists have developed new ways of debugging. One of them is to heat or freeze a building. The bugs inside the house die from the extreme temperatures. This method keeps poisons out of the air and saves all the trees it would have taken to build new wooden buildings.

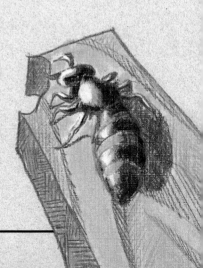

SKEETER SCAT

Mosquitoes can really ruin an outdoor event. They swarm in, and everyone runs for some spray. But here are some healthier ideas for beating the bugs:
• Wear Avon's Skin-So-Soft™ lotion. It smells good and makes you less tasty to mosquitoes.
• Have someone light candles made of citronella near your table. Mosquitoes don't like the citronella smell.
• Plant citrosa on your porch or patio. This new type of plant from Holland has the citronella scent right in the leaves.

MICE MENACE

Most people don't like to live with mice or squirrels in their homes. So if you don't have a cat to chase them away, and you don't want to use deadly poisons or traps, you can get animal-friendly traps. These traps catch the animals but don't hurt them. Then you can take the animals into the country and set them loose outside. You can find animal-friendly traps at the Humane Society near you.

INVITE A BAT TO YOUR BARBECUE

One bat eats 600 mosquitoes every hour. While you eat your dinner, bats will keep the mosquitoes from eating you. Don't worry about the bats bothering you. They are very shy. (By the way, it's a myth that bats like to fly into people's hair. It's also untrue that a lot of bats carry rabies. Very few do.) To encourage bats to live near you, put up a bat house in a high tree trunk. To find out more about bats and bat houses, write to:
Bat Conservation
International
P. O. Box 162603
Austin, TX 78716

Power Choices

Turned-On Homes

What makes your lights go on,
your oven heat up,
and your TV run?
Electricity.
Electricity makes our lives
cozy and comfortable.
But what makes electricity?
Most electricity these days
is made in only a few ways:
by burning coal, oil, or gas;
by burning garbage; by river
water turning water wheels;
or through nuclear processes.
All these ways to make electric
energy can be harmful to the earth.
Burning coal, oil, gas, and garbage
puts sickening smoke in the air.
Mining for coal can strip the land
of trees and other plants.
Then the rich top layer of soil is
left to wash or blow away.
Mining also causes
water pollution.

Shipping oil can lead
to large oil spills.
The dams needed for water
wheels change rivers so much it
hurts the animals that live there.
Nuclear energy seems clean,
but it makes wastes that are
deadly to touch or be near.
And these wastes last hundreds
of thousands of years.
So what do we do?
We can make electricity
in other ways
that are kinder to the earth.
But until we do this more,
the best answer is to conserve
energy—to save energy by cutting
back on the electricity we use.

CONSERVING EVERY DAY

*Here are a few ways you can conserve energy with-
out throwing all your appliances out the window.*
- *Turn off the lights when you leave a room.*
- *Turn off radios, TVs, stereos,
tape players, and VCRs
when you are done
with them.*

- *If you help with the laundry,
let your clothes dry on a line
instead of using a clothes dryer.*
- *During the summer, close
your windows, shades, and
curtains in the morning
(except a crack to let your
plants get some sun).
This keeps the sun from
heating your rooms.
Then open your win-
dows at night to let in cool
breezes. If you have air
conditioning, shut it off
when no one is home or at
night, when it's cool outside.*
- *When you help cook, use a
hand-run mixer or can opener
instead of electric ones.*
- *For free information on new
technology for conserving
energy, write to:*
  Alliance to Save Energy
  1725 K Street Northwest
  Suite 509
  Washington, DC 20006

- *During the winter, open your
shades and curtains in the
morning so the sun can heat
up your rooms. Then at dusk,
shut them to keep the heat in.*
- *Enjoy the "layered look." It's
fashionable to wear sweaters
and sweatshirts during the fall,
winter, and early spring. If
you're dressed up, you can
turn the heat down to 65°F.
At night when you're all
snuggled under the covers,
or when no one is home, the
heat can be turned down even
lower—to 58°F. Keeping the
temperature low is healthy for
you too. Most germs grow
faster at 70-80°F than at
58-69°F.*
- *Put a reminder note on
the dishwasher that says:
Please fill me up before
using, and stop me before
the drying cycle—the air
will dry your dishes.*

Rate Your Place

To find out how much
you depend on electricity,
go on a home-energy hunt.
First, guess how many things in
your home need electricity to run.
10? 20? 50?
Write down your guess.
Now walk in and out of every
room, counting
up all the
lightbulbs.

Next count the appliances—
toasters, TVs, vacuum cleaners,
VCRs, fans, clothes dryers,
air conditioners, computers,
freezers, can openers,
hair dryers, and mixers.
Don't forget the clocks and
radios—add them to your total.
Is your final count a lot higher
than your first guess?
Are you surprised at how many
plug-in things you rely on
in your house?

COAL COUNTDOWN

Too much carbon dioxide
in the air can be harmful to the
planet. Many electric power plants
burn coal and give off smoke with carbon
dioxide in it. So when we use electricity, we are
often adding to the amount of carbon dioxide
in the sky. Here is a chart showing how many
pounds of carbon dioxide can go into the air
when you use certain electrical appliances:

Color TV	1 hour	.64 lbs.
100-watt lightbulb	10 hours	1.29 lbs.
Vacuum cleaner	1 hour	1.70 lbs.
Clothes dryer	1 load	10.00 lbs.
Refrigerator	1 day	12.80 lbs.

COOL BULBS

We use two kinds of lightbulbs in our homes: incandescent and fluorescent. Fluorescent bulbs are the more energy efficient. It takes less electricity (fewer watts) to run them. A 15-watt compact fluorescent bulb lights up a room just as brightly as a 75-watt incandescent bulb. And the fluorescent bulb lasts 10 times longer. (It costs a little more too, but the bulb pays for itself in energy savings.)

If every household in the U.S. replaced just one 100-watt incandescent lightbulb with a 13-watt compact fluorescent bulb, we could stop about 29 million tons of carbon dioxide per year from being put into the air by coal-burning power plants. Now that would make a difference.

ENERGY ARITHMETIC

Q: How much energy do you think the average person in the U.S. uses in a year?

A: The average American uses so much energy that a coal-burning power plant would have to burn up 80 pounds of coal to make that much electricity. Think of all that smoke.

Q: How much dangerous waste from nuclear power plants is stored in the U.S.?

A: At least 18,000 tons. That's more than the weight of about 3,000 male African elephants. And because nuclear waste causes cancer and other illnesses, no one wants any of this waste stored nearby. So the more we can conserve energy, the less people will depend on nuclear power.

The Sky's the Limit

How can we make electricity
without damaging the world?
By working with nature:
the sun, the wind, the plants,
the earth's heat,
and the oceans' tides.
These are called renewable
energy sources because
they can't be used up.
Scientists and engineers have
come up with creative inventions
to use renewable energy sources.
Windmills, solar
batteries (sun-
powered), and
geothermal
heaters
(powered by
the earth's heat)
are just some of
these inventions.

Electricity made from renewable
energy sources usually
costs less over the years
than electricity made by
nuclear or coal-burning
power plants.
The United States Department
of Energy says that almost ¾
of the nation's energy could come
from renewable sources.

NEW WAVES

*Can ocean waves be used to make
clean, safe electricity for a whole
town? The people in Islay, Scotland,
hope so. Their village is on the
Atlantic coast where waves beat
against the rocks night and day.
Engineers are testing a power plant
that turns the wave energy into
electricity for the town. Until now,
Islay has used oil to make its
electricity.*

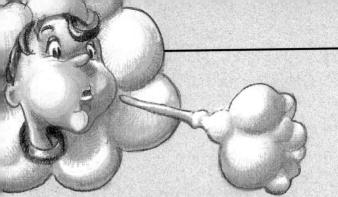

BLOW, WIND, BLOW

Can you imagine a field filled with windmills? They are called windmill farms. Some experts say that if there were windmill farms across the nation, the farms could supply nearly ½ of our entire energy needs. Many farmers and home-owners have their own windmills. Some of these windmills work so well that these people have extra power to sell. They sell the electricity to the local power company for other people's homes.

Windmills used to make electricity in southern Minnesota

THE HEAT'S ON

The sun provides about 100,000 times the energy of all the world's power plants combined.

SUN PARK

The city of Austin, Texas, has a solar-powered parking ramp. The solar cells on the top of the ramp make enough electricity during the day to light up the ramp at night. The parking ramp also makes enough electricity to power 100 homes.

MAGNETIC TRAINS

Did you know that mag-nets can pull steel? In Japan, people have put that power to work. They have built trains that are pulled along their tracks by powerful magnets. The trains use very little electricity to run.

Try experiments that help you understand the way renewable energy sources work, and share them with your family. (Solar-power experiments are some of the easiest.)
If you have questions about renewable energy, call the hotline of the Careers, Conservation and Renewable Energy Inquiry and Referral Service at 1-800-523-2929.

Energetic Kids

Would you like to work for renewable energy?
The first thing to do is to learn more about it.
Check out books at the library.
Ask the librarian to help you find articles in magazines.

SUNNY SOLUTIONS

Sun power is not new. Back in 1897, almost ⅓ of the homes in Pasadena, California, used solar water heaters. These days you don't even have to live in a place with hot weather to have the sun work for you. If you want a packet of information on solar energy and experiments you can do, write to:

Florida Solar Energy Center
300 State Road, #401
Cape Canaveral, FL 32920

SOLAR TEA

Try an experiment using the sun's heat instead of your stove's heat to make tea. On a sunny day, fill a gallon jar with water and add four tea bags. Leave the jar in the sun until the tea is as dark as you like it. Mix in some honey and ice, and you have sun tea.

HOT ENOUGH TO FRY AN EGG

You've heard about sidewalks getting hot enough to cook on. Now you can make this heat work for you. Take a cardboard box with a tilt-off lid (like a bakery cake box). Cover the insides of the box and the lid with aluminum foil (shiny side up). Paint the outsides and the bottom of the inside black.

On a hot, sunny day, prop the lid open with a stick, and face the lid toward the sun. Now try cooking different foods in your oven. Try an egg. How long does it take to fry? Try a hotdog. (You'll have to keep turning it.) How about vegetables in butter or a grilled cheese sandwich? Have fun experimenting, but make sure you don't leave your food, or some dog, cat, or squirrel might snatch your lunch.

HOME, SOLAR HOME

Joyce Ford and Jim Riddle have a farm near Winona, Minnesota. All the electricity for their home comes from the sun. They use solar energy to run their answering machine, computer, lights, stereo, and TV. They store their food in a root cellar and cook meals on a wood stove. They also use a composting toilet and heat their home with their stove.

Smart Shopping

What's Eating You?

Some foods are healthier for us
than others.
And some foods are better
for the planet than others.
Grocery stores carry
both kinds of food.
We can learn to make
smart choices for our bodies
and for the planet.
With a little information,
it's easy to eat in an earthwise way.

EAT LESS MEAT?

Many people say there are good reasons to eat less meat—especially beef. Most hamburgers and steaks are made of beef. Thousands of acres of forest, including rain forest, are cut down each year to raise food for beef cattle. In addition, many animals that are raised for meat live their whole lives in small pens and are often fed unnecessary chemicals. We eat these chemicals when we eat the meat. So when or if your family eats meat, ask your parents to buy meat from local farmers who don't use chemicals and don't keep their animals in small pens. The names and addresses of these farmers can often be found at your local co-op.

TRAVELING TOMATOES

If you've eaten a tomato lately, it's probably traveled more than you have. The average piece of food eaten in America has traveled 1,300 miles. That's a lot of gas wasted on a tomato. For this reason, it's good to buy foods that are grown in your area.

GO ORGANIC

If you want safe foods to eat—ones that haven't been sprayed with chemicals—buy food items that say "organic" on the labels. The food might cost a little more, but this food won't make you or the planet sick.

You can grow your own organic herbs and vegetables in used plastic containers in a window or in a garden. Some cities even rent garden plots. Your family may want to try gardening together. It can be great fun to watch your plants grow. And the harvest is extremely tasty!

RAIN-FOREST SWEETS

The world's rain forests are being cut for timber and burned to make room for farms. But more money and jobs can come from a living forest than a dead one.

Brazil-nut trees are the largest trees in the southern rain forests. Collecting and using the nuts from these trees makes more jobs and five times more money than cutting the trees for timber or farming. You can encourage people to stop killing the trees by buying rain-forest nuts and foods made with them. One good choice is Rainforest Crunch candy (it's delicious!). You can find it in many stores or buy it from:

Community Products, Inc.
RD #2, Box 1950
Montpelier, VT 05602
(This company buys its nuts from small companies run by forest peoples.)

SHOP CO-OP

Food co-ops are grocery stores where the shoppers work together to run the business. These stores usually carry only products that are good for the earth. They have organic fruits and vegetables, recycled products, energy-efficient light bulbs, and natural cleaners. For the name and address of the co-op closest to you, write to:

National Cooperative
  Business Institute
1401 New York Avenue NW
Suite 1100
Washington, DC 20005

FOOD SHELF

Part of learning to be earthwise is learning to care for every living being on the planet. In every town and city, there are people who are hungry. When you and your family go shopping, you might want to buy food for people who don't have much money, if you can. Then take those items to your neighborhood food shelf. People who can't afford to buy food come to food shelves to get good things for their families to eat.

BAG IT!

Q: When you go to a store, is it best to choose a paper bag or a plastic one?

A: This is a trick question. The answer is neither. It's best to bring your own bag of cloth, string, or netting. You can use the bag over and over instead of throwing it away. Also, cellophane (which is made from plants and is biodegradable) and aluminum foil (which is recyclable) are better than plastic wrap. Avoid things wrapped or packaged individually—even juice boxes and squeeze bottles. Remember where they end up!

Peppers $1.25

Table Grapes 30¢/lb

REFILLABLE VS. RECYCLABLE

It takes less energy to wash out an old container and use it again than to recycle and make a new one. So look for beverages, shampoos, and other products that come in large, refillable containers. Containers that can be used over and over again are even better than recyclable ones!

TO MARKET, TO MARKET

Farmers' markets are also good places to shop. These are neighborhood areas where many people set up tables and sell homegrown fruits, vegetables, and flowers as well as homemade baked goods and crafts. For the address of a farmers' market near you, write to:

Project for Public
    Spaces, Inc.
153 Waverly Place
New York, NY 10014

ALL PRODUCE Sold HERE HOME GROWN in AUBURN WASH.

HOMEMADE IS IN!

People used to think that things made in a factory were better than things made at home. That's not true now. Shoppers pay high prices for handmade and homemade items. See what things you can learn to make: foods, clothes, presents, greeting cards, bird houses and feeders, and other things. Use your imagination. There are many books in the library that can give you ideas and directions.

Planet-Friendly Products

Sometimes it may seem like we can't do anything about factories, farms, and companies that are polluting the earth. But we really can.

We can encourage businesses to be earthwise by choosing to buy as many things as possible from businesses that *are* being careful about how they treat the planet.

At the same time, we can try not to buy from businesses that aren't.

RECYCLED AND RECYCLABLE

*If you want businesses to make products out of recycled materials, you need to buy these kinds of products. An easy place to start is with paper. This symbol, with a circle around it, will appear on the label of items that are **made of recycled materials**. These are the best paper products for the environment.*

AQUA FRIENDLY

Shampoos, dish soap, and other cleaners often have chemicals in them that are called phosphates. Phosphates can ruin a river or lake. So when you are helping your parents shop, ask them to buy products that say "No phosphates" and "biodegradable." These labels mean that the products won't pollute water.

If a tuna product says it is "dolphin-safe," it should mean that no dolphins were caught or killed in the fishing nets. The "Flipper Seal of Approval" is awarded to companies that help protect dolphins in many ways.

Also watch for labels saying that a product is "animal-friendly" or "cruelty-free." These words mean that no animals were treated badly to make or test the product.

This symbol means a product is **recyclable**—you can throw it into the recycling bin when you are done with it. Be careful not to confuse this symbol with the "made of recycled materials" symbol. Recyclable goods are often not made of recycled materials.

This acid-free symbol means that a product has been made without using dangerous acids. Look for paper products with this sign on it. Also look for paper products that say "chlorine-free."

Blue Angel in Germany

Environmental Choice in Canada

Green Seal in the United States of America

Eco Mark in Japan

GREEN MARKS THE SPOT

To help people make good choices when they shop, some groups are making seals of approval to put on the labels of products. These symbols tell you that a certain product is the best available choice (or one of the best) to protect the planet. Different countries have different environmental seals of approval.

BUSINESSES TAKE THE PLEDGE!

Many businesses have signed a pledge to try to care for the earth. This pledge is made up of several promises and guidelines called the Valdez Principles. When you can, buy products from companies that have promised to follow these principles. You can find out if a company follows them by writing and asking the company.

You don't have to wait until you are grown up and have a company of your own to start practicing the Valdez Principles. You can start right now. Whenever you do a job to earn money, you can pledge to do it in a way that enriches and cares for the earth.

SONGS TO SAVE THE EARTH

A popular rock group in Australia called Midnight Oil sings about the dangers facing our planet. Their albums, such as Blue Sky Mining, urge listeners to do something before it is too late. Other musicians, like Sting and Sweet Honey in the Rock, are singing about similar concerns.

COMPANY CLUES

If your family would like to buy a guide on how to shop for a better world, write to:
Council on Economic Priorities
30 Irving Place
New York, NY 10003

Some Spots to Shop

If your family is looking for planet-friendly products, here are some mail-order stores that have them. Write and ask for a catalog.

Appel Co. Cleaners
1500 West Hampton, 5F
Englewood, CO 80110

BAU
Interior and Exterior Paints
P. O. Box 190
Alton, NH 03809

The Body Shop
Skin and Hair Care
  Preparations
45 Horsehill Road
Cedar Knolls, NJ 07927

Earth Care Paper, Inc.
P. O. Box 7070
Madison, WI 53707

Earth Wise
Cleaning Products
Consumer Services
4600 Sleepy Time Drive
Boulder, CO 80301

Eco Source
P. O. Box 1656
Sebastopol, CA 95473

Gardener's Supply
128 Intervale Road
Burlington, VT 05401

The Green Market
118 Prospect Blvd.
St. Paul, MN 55107

Jade Mountain
P. O. Box 4616
Boulder, CO 80306-4616

The Natural Choice
1365 Rufima Circle
Santa Fe, NM 87501

Mia Rosa Products
177-F Riverside Ave.
Newport Beach, CA 92663

Real Goods Trading Co.
966 Mazzoni Street
Ukiah, CA 95482

Ringer Corporation
Chemical-Free Lawn
  and Garden Care
9959 Valley View Road
Eden Prairie, MN 55344

Rising Sun Enterprises
P. O. Box 1728
Basalt, CO 81621

Save Energy Company
2410 Harrison Street
San Francisco, CA 94110

Seventh Generation
49 Hercules Drive
Colchester, VT 05446

Solar Box Cookers
  International
1724 11th Street
Sacramento, CA 95814

Solar Survival Architects
Earth Ships
P.O. Box 1041
Taos, NM 87571

Sunergy
Solar Products
P. O. Box 177
Princeton, NJ 08542

Where Do We Go from Here?

On the Move

Our earthwise search has just begun. In our neighborhoods, cities, and counties, there are many people we can talk to for more information. It's good to find out many people's opinions and solutions to problems. Here are just some of the places to visit, people to talk to, and organizations to contact:

Alternative Energy Society
Audubon Society (local)
City council members
Co-op workers
County commissioners
Environmental groups (local)
Environmental Protection
 Agency (EPA)
Environment Canada
Factories
Farmers' markets
Farmers
Food-shelf workers
Garbage burners
Goodwill stores
Government representatives
Greenpeace (local)
Grocery-store owners

Hazardous-waste
 drop-off centers
Homeless shelters
Landfills
Libraries
Nature centers
Organic gardeners
Papermaking plants
Power companies
Trash collectors
Salvation Army workers
Pollution Control Agencies
 (local)
Recycling companies
Repair shops
Sierra Club (local)
Used clothing shops
Water-treatment plants
Windmill farms

You can also read the other two books in the earthwise series: *Earthwise at Play* and *Earthwise at School*.